Imprint:
HF Publishing

ISBN: 979-8-9879431-0-6
ISBN: 979-8-9879431-1-3 (ebook)

Thank you to Emma & Laura

We have printed this book in black and white to keep the price down for you. You can find color photos plus additional ones at:

dmdcookbook.com

DAD MAKES
DINNER
AND OTHER MEALS, TOO
COOKBOOK

Simple and Delicious Kid Approved Recipes

Michael Faeth

Photos by Emma Faeth

Contents

Introduction

Inside of this book you will get 17 essential recipes that you can use over and over to make simple meals your kids will absolutely love. You will find helpful tips and if there is a particular product that works well with the recipe, you will find recommendations, too.

We try and purchase organic products as much as possible. Our favorite places to shop include our local farmers market, Trader Joe's, and Whole Foods. I use a lot of olive oil when I cook. I mean, a lot! I once heard Julia Child say you need a certain amount of fat in your diet to process your vitamins. Olive oil, along with avocados and salmon, is how I prefer to get it. A lot of the recipes included are right in line with a Mediterranean diet. After researching what foods might help with boosting immunity, I discovered the benefits of mushrooms. I cook with them to support good health and to add extra umami. My daughter prefers no mushrooms at this point, so I just take them out when I make her plate. We use mainly whole wheat bread, tortillas, and pasta.

The right amount of salt and pepper can make a huge difference in flavor. When it comes to measuring, I almost always eyeball amounts. Most measurements included in the recipes are general estimates, so experiment with those. An exception is the recipe for the New Fashioned Pancakes, so follow that more closely. Most of these recipes make one or two servings, so adjust them as needed.

Have fun cooking with your kids and teach them about kitchen safety. Help them learn the importance of a healthy diet and how to cook for themselves. We hope you find some new meals to enjoy together with your family and loved ones.

Eat well and be well,
Michael

BREAKFAST

Soft Fried Egg

Savory Turkey Sausage Links

Fabulous Frittata

Organic Cinnamon Sugar Toast

New Fashioned Pancakes

Soft Fried Egg

This simple recipe is a cross between a fried egg and scrambled eggs. I have watched the master chef Jacques Pépin make eggs and he cooks them to be soft and creamy. I attempt to cook them just enough so they are no longer raw but before becoming rubbery.

Ingredients

Egg

Extra Virgin Olive Oil

Salt & Pepper

Tools

A small cast iron pan works perfectly, but use any pan you have, and a fork.

Prepare

Put a small amount of salt and pepper into your pan and turn the heat to medium-high. Add a small amount of olive oil (around 1 tbsp) and move the pan around to coat the bottom and sides.

Once pan is hot, crack the egg in. Wait until the egg starts to turn white, take the fork and break the yolk and start to slowly turn the egg over. Do this until the egg is somewhat mixed together and cooked very softly throughout. Plate the egg and let sit for about minute so the egg continues to cook before enjoying.

Recommendation

Buy cage free brown or white eggs.

TIP: To clean cast iron pans, wipe with paper towel when cool. Heat and carefully rinse with water over the sink. I store ours in the oven. For stainless steel, fill with water when cooled and let soak a couple of hours for easy cleaning.

Savory Turkey Sausage Links

The thing that makes pork sausage so flavorful is the fat. Since turkey is leaner, there isn't much fat. I use olive oil and water to create a rich sauce that elevates the flavor to the level that even a pork sausage lover will appreciate.

Ingredients

Frozen Turkey Sausage Links

Extra Virgin Olive Oil

Salt & Pepper

Filtered Water

Tools

A small stainless steel pan with a lid works perfectly, but use any pan you have.

Prepare

Put a small amount of salt and pepper into your pan and turn the heat to medium-high. Add a small amount of olive oil (around 1 tbsp) and add the sausage. Heat until sausage is coated and starts to brown. Turn the heat down to low and after a minute or so, add about 2 tbsp of water, swirl the pan around to emulsify the water and oil the best you can, put the lid on and let simmer for about 2 minutes.

Plate the sausage and let sit for a minute before enjoying.

Product Recommendation

Jones Dairy Farm® Turkey Sausage Links (or patties)

TIP: Turn the heat down before adding the water to minimize splattering. Swirl the pan to emulsify the oil and water the best you can before covering and simmering.

Fabulous Frittata

Here is a delicious dish that will make for a very special breakfast. There are several steps involved but it is well worth the wait to enjoy the rich flavors.

Ingredients

Two Eggs

Extra Virgin Olive Oil

Salt & Pepper

2 tbsp Milk

1/4 cup Red Bell Pepper

1/4 cup Cooked Potatoes

1/4 cup Cheddar or Mozzarella

2 tbsp Parmesan Cheese

1 Slice of Turkey Bacon

Tools

A small cast iron pans works perfectly, but use any oven proof pan you have, cutting board, paring knife, and
a whisk

Prepare

Boil potatoes until soft but still firm, cool, and chop into small squares. Chop bell pepper and cheese into small pieces. Crack two eggs into a bowl, add the milk, Parmesan, and cheese and whisk together.

Put a salt and pepper into your pan and turn the heat to medium-high. Add turkey bacon and cut into small pieces as it cooks. After about a minute, add a small amount of olive oil (around 1 tbsp) and add the chopped bell pepper and potatoes. Continue to cook until lightly browned, add in the egg mixture, and stir.

Continue cooking on the stove until the egg near the sides of the pan becomes a little firm. Then transfer the pan to the oven and bake at 375 degrees until egg is cooked, about 15 minutes. Stick a toothpick into the center to test to see if the egg is cooked all the way through.

Let cool slightly, cut into quarters, and plate to enjoy.

Organic Cinnamon Sugar Toast

This simple breakfast was one of the first foods I fell in love with as a kid. I still love making it. Pair it with a cold glass of milk.

Ingredients

Organic Whole Wheat Bread

Organic Cinnamon

Organic White Sugar

Organic Butter

Tools

A toaster, small glass jar, a spoon, and a butter knife.

Prepare

Mix 1 tbsp of cinnamon with 2 1/2 tbsp of white sugar in small glass jar.

Toast the bread to the darkness you prefer. I like the toast on the dark and crunchy side. Butter the toast generously, and then sprinkle a generous amount of the cinnamon and sugar mixture on the toast.

New Fashioned Pancakes

Here is a new spin on a classic. The addition of the spices and vanilla is subtle but adds a complexity to the flavor. Top this with organic real maple syrup, butter, and a dusting of powder sugar.

Ingredients

3/4 cups organic white flour

3/4 cups organic wheat flour

3 1/2 teaspoons baking powder

1 tsp salt

1 tbsp white sugar

1 1/4 cup organic milk

1 egg

3 tbsp olive oil

1 dash nutmeg

1 tsp cinnamon

1/2 tsp vanilla

Real Maple Syrup

Butter

Powdered Sugar

Tools

Cast iron pan, mixing spoon, bowl, spatula, butter knife, and sieve

Prepare

Mix dry ingredients in a bowl. Add milk, olive oil, and vanilla and mix all ingredients into a thick but easily pourable batter. Heat the pan to medium-high and add a small slab of butter. When melted, pour enough batter in to make a 3 to 4 inch pancake. Brown lightly on both sides and plate. Repeat with each pancake you make. Finish with butter, pure maple syrup, and a dusting of powdered sugar.

Use the same batter in a waffle iron to make: **New Fashioned Waffles**

Replace the milk with a 12oz bottle of beer to make: **Beer Pancakes**

For a classic recipe, search "Good Old Fashioned Pancakes" at: allrecipes.com

TIP: Make the batter a little early and let it sit for at least 20 minutes before making pancakes. First flip the pancake after bubbles have formed. If the cast iron pan becomes too hot and smoky, carefully take it to the sink and rinse with water.

LUNCH

Peanut Butter & Jam Sandwich

Grilled Cheese Sandwich

Black Bean Quesarrito

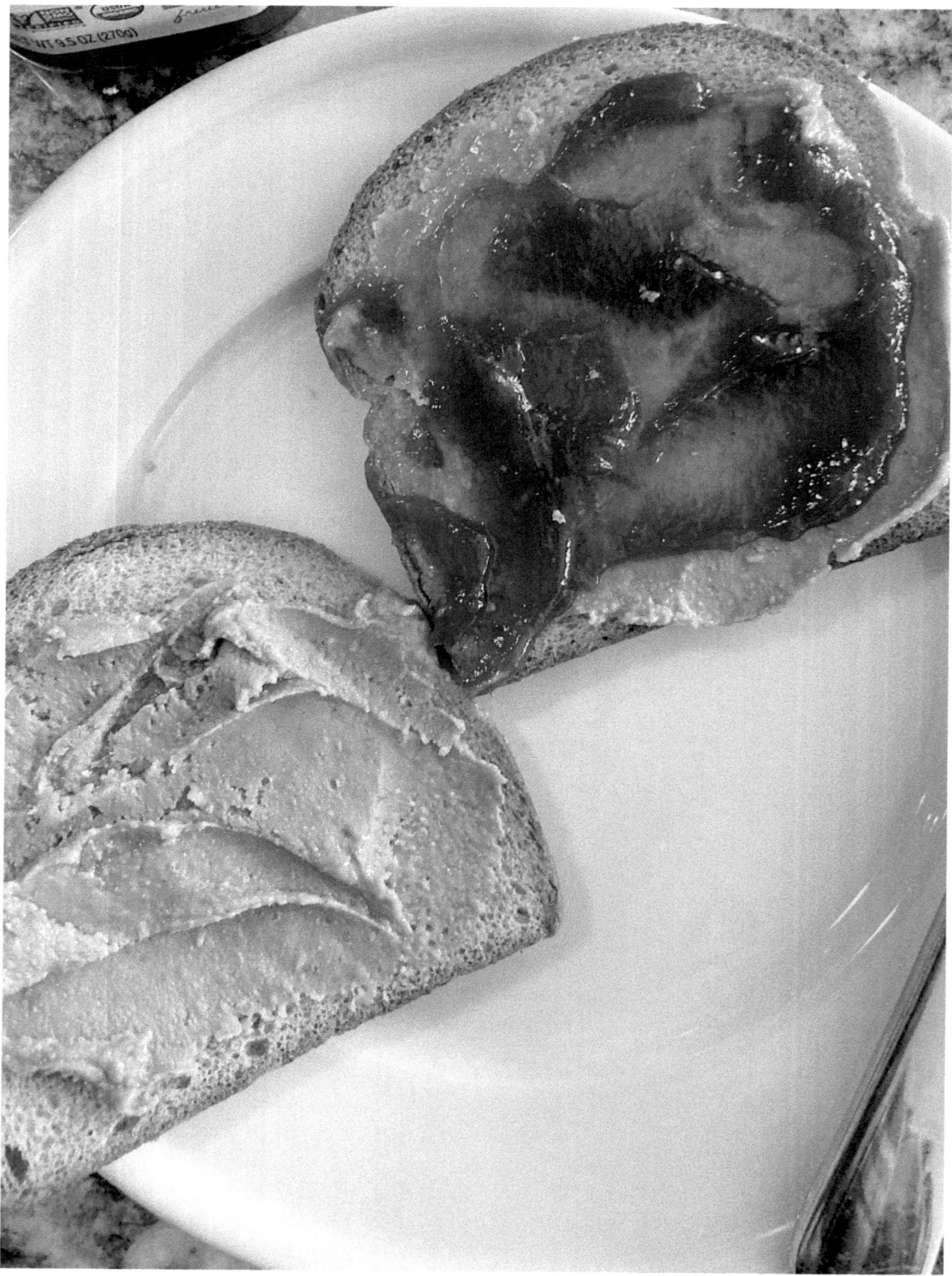

Peanut Butter & Jam Sandwich

Hard to find a more classic sandwich than a PB&J. In this case, the "J" stands for jam and all of the ingredients are organic.

Ingredients

Organic Whole Wheat Bread

Organic Peanut Butter

Organic Raspberry Jam

Organic Potato Chips

Tools

A spoon and a butter knife.

Prepare

Spread a thin layer of peanut butter on both pieces of bread. This helps to keep the jam from absorbing into the bread (especially if you are packing a school lunch). Add the jam and stack into a sandwich. Serve with a side of potato chips. A cold glass of milk is a perfect compliment.

Recommendations

Santa Cruz Organics Creamy Peanut Butter

Santa Cruz Organics Seedless Red Raspberry Jam

TIP: Store peanut butter jar upside down for about 2-3 weeks before opening it. The oil will move to the bottom of the jar making it easier to stir. Store in refrigerator and take out 10 minutes before using to let it soften. Avoid buying "No Stir" types because they have other ingredients added.

Grilled Cheese Sandwich

Here is a favorite for kids and adults alike. This is a great comfort food that always pleases. To make a variation, add Dijon mustard and thinly sliced tomatoes.

Ingredients

Whole Wheat Bread

Organic Sharp Cheddar Cheese

Extra Virgin Olive Oil

Salt & Pepper

BBQ Chips

Small Carrot

Tools

Cast iron or non-stick pan, paring knife, cutting board, and a spatula or fork
for flipping.

Prepare

Make enough thin slices of cheese to cover one piece of bread. Salt and pepper the pan, heat to medium-high, and add about 2-3 tbsp of olive oil. When hot, put both piece of bread in the pan and top one slice with the cheese. After the cheese visibly softens, flip the other piece of bread on top of the slice with the cheese. You should see some browning to the bread. Continue to flip the entire sandwich over until both sides are golden brown and the cheese is melted. Serve with BBQ chips and sliced carrots.

Recommendation

Rumiano Organic Sharp Cheddar Cheese

TIP: Wait until the pan is hot before putting the bread in to help it not stick. Put both pieces of bread into the pan so they can start to brown, adding the cheese to one slice of bread.

Black Bean Quesarrito

When I was living in Seattle, my friend David came up from California to visit. Instead of making traditional burritos, David put tortillas and cheese in a cast iron pan like a quesadilla and then added refried beans. This recipe is a variation.

Ingredients

Whole Wheat Tortillas

Black Beans

Cheddar Cheese

Avocado

Salsa

Extra Virgin Olive Oil

Salt & Pepper

Corn Chips

Tools

Cast iron pan or any you have, paring knife, cutting board, spoon, and a spatula or fork for flipping

Prepare

Add salt and pepper along with about 2 table spoons of olive oil into your pan on medium heat. Place two tortillas down flat into the pan (they might overlap a little in the middle) and add small amounts of black beans, cheese, avocado, and salsa. When you see the cheese starting to melt, fold the tortillas over so they fit nicely into the pan. Continue cooking until the tortillas are golden brown on both sides. Cut each into two or three pieces and let cool a few minute before eating. Serve with corn chips.

Recommendations

Trader Joe's ® Organic Blue Corn Tortilla Chips

TIP: After they are done cooking, cut each into 2 or 3 pieces and let them cool a little. This makes them easier to eat and helps them from being too messy.

DINNER

Chicken Tenders & French Fries

Red Sauce Penne Pasta

Charcoal Grilled Salmon, Bread & Squash

Chicken Tenders & French Fries

While you could run down to the corner fast food restaurant and pick up nuggets and fries, staying home and making your own is going to be easy and probably healthier and better tasting. Pair this with BBQ sauce and ketchup.

Ingredients

2 or 3 Chicken Breast Tenders (per person)

French Fries

Salt & Pepper

BBQ Sauce

Ketchup

Tools

Toaster oven or regular oven, parchment paper, and a cookie sheet

Prepare

Pre-heat oven to 425° as you get your cookie sheet ready with the tenders and fries. Bake in oven for about 20 minutes. Serve with ketchup and BBQ sauce.

Recommendations

Yummy® Chicken Breast Tenders

Sprouts® Organic Bourbon BBQ Sauce*

Primal Kitchen® Ketchup Organic and Unsweetened**

Sprouts® Organic Steak Fries

*This BBQ sauce is deliciously tangy with just a slight bit of heat

**I prefer ketchup in a glass jar as opposed to a plastic bottle. I have fond memories of glass bottles of Heinz® ketchup and it is hard to beat that flavor, but this is a good alternative and plus it is organic.

TIP: Put down parchment paper on your cookie sheet for easy clean up.

Red Sauce Penne Pasta

Pasta always hits the spot. When I worked in an Italian restaurant I learned about placing the pasta right into the pan with the sauce, as opposed to ladling sauce over cooked pasta. This allows for the pasta to get coated with sauce and assures a very hot plate of pasta.

Ingredients

2-3 Handfuls of Penne Pasta

About 1 cup Marinara Sauce

2-3 tbsp Extra Virgin Olive Oil

Salt & Pepper

Parmesan

2 Mushrooms

Filtered Water

Tools

Pan with lid, fork or spoon, paring knife, cutting board

Prepare

Add a liberal amount of salt to water in a pan, cover with lid, and heat to a boil. Add penne and cook 11-13 minutes without lid, stirring occasionally, until al dente (cooked but still firm). To test firmness, use a fork or spoon and press a piece of pasta against the side of the pan. Drain water using the lid and keep pasta in the pan. Turn down the heat, add olive oil and mushrooms and stir to coat with oil. Add sauce and salt and pepper, turn heat back up, and stir until pasta is hot and well coated with sauce. Plate and serve with Parmesan on top. You can drizzle a little more olive oil on top, if desired.

TIP: Use the "bachelor" method of cooking and do everything in one pan. Use the lid to drain the water and keep the pasta in the pan. Add the olive oil, salt and pepper, and mushrooms before eventually adding the sauce.

Charcoal Grilled Salmon, Bread & Squash

Grilled salmon is one of my favorite foods. This recipe is modeled after the way salmon is often grilled in the NW. It involves several steps, but is very worth the effort.

Ingredients

Atlantic Salmon Boneless Fillets w/ Skin
Extra Virgin Olive Oil
Garlic Salt & Pepper
Fresh Lemon
Yellow Squash
Round Bread Loaf

Tools

Charcoal Grill (I use 18" Weber), Charcoal Chimney Starter, Hardwood Charcoal, Dry Paper, Grilling Tongs, Grill Brush, Foil, Paring Knife, and Cutting Board

Prepare

Garlic salt and pepper a clean plate and drizzle with about a tbsp of olive oil. Place salmon flesh down on the plate and move around to coat. Flip over and get skin side right before grilling. Slice bread into about 1" slices and yellow squash into long strips. Liberally apply olive oil, garlic salt, and pepper.

Place charcoal into chimney and then fill bottom with dry paper. Open vents at bottom of BBQ, remove grill and place chimney inside to light. Let burn for about 5 minutes until charcoal is nice and hot, turn over and pour onto one side of the BBQ. Replace grill, let charcoal burn without lid on for a few more minutes and then put lid on with vents open at top. After grill is entirely hot, remove lid, clean grill with brush.

Place salmon fillet flesh down directly over charcoal. Let sear for about 2-4 minutes. Spin grill so salmon is above cooler area and put lid back on. Cook another 5-7 minutes. Remove lid, spin salmon back to hot side. Using tongs slowly lift sides of salmon off of the grill. Be patient and continue prying salmon off of the grill and it should eventually come free without sticking. Flip over and repeat grilling steps (maybe slightly less time). After salmon is fully cooked (fat appears white at edges, center is very hot, and fish easily flakes apart), put on clean plate and cover tightly with aluminum foil. Let sit while you finish grilling (or at least 5 minutes before serving). Serve with lemon squeezed on top. Grill bread to golden brown and squash until hot all the way through.

> TIP: To minimize smoke, don't over stuff the chimney with paper to get a quick and hot flame. Store tongs and brush in the charcoal once cool and clean tongs with brush next time. Put hot coals on one side to have a hot zone and cool zone. Spin the grill to move salmon to zones. Use tongs and easily rotate the fillet to help break it free. Be sure to cook thoroughly. Cut your yellow squash into long quarters and grill them perpendicularly to the grill bars.

VEGETABLES

Cauliflower Simmered in Broth

Sautéed Sweet Peas & Mushrooms

Sautéed Baby Spinach & Garlic

Cauliflower Simmered in Broth

Is it sometimes challenging to get your kids to eat vegetables? Give this recipe a shot! It involves slow simmering in broth with olive oil, black pepper, and mushrooms. This method can be used to cook different types of vegetables, too.

Ingredients

About 1 tsp Broth Base
(see recommendations)

1-2 cups Cauliflower

1-2 tbsp Extra Virgin Olive Oil

Black Pepper

1-2 Mushrooms

3/4-1 cup Filtered Water

Tools

Pan with a lid, spoon, paring knife, cutting board

Prepare

Heat olive oil in a pan on medium heat and add crushed black pepper. Add sliced mushroom and cauliflower and move around to coat with oil. Pour in water and after heated, stir in the broth base. The trick is to get just the right amount of base to water ratio. If too much, the broth will be salty; too little, it will be unsavory. The directions call for 1 tsp per 1 cup of water, but experiment until you get the right amount of broth and the flavor you like. Once the broth is mixed in, cover and let simmer until cauliflower is tender but not too soft, about 3 to 5 minutes. Serve on a plate with or without the mushrooms, pouring a little bit of broth over the top. I put mine in a bowl and finish the broth.

You can make broccoli, Brussels sprouts, asparagus, and sweet corn the same way. Pair these vegetables with the lunch and dinner recipes.

Recommendations

Better Than Bouillon® Organic Seasoned Vegetable Base

Better Than Bouillon® Organic Roasted Chicken Base

TIP: No need to use salt in this recipe since it comes from the broth. You can use vegetable or chicken broth.

Sautéed Sweet Peas & Mushrooms

Looking for a super easy way to add vegetables to a meal? Simple pull a bag of frozen peas from the freezer and one mushroom from the fridge. Then sauté them with olive oil and salt and pepper. Getting the right amount of salt will really bring out the flavor.

Ingredients

1 cup Frozen Peas

1 tsp Extra Virgin Olive Oil

1 Mushroom

Salt & Pepper

Tools

Small cast iron pan or any pan you have, spoon, paring knife, cutting board

Prepare

Cut a clean mushroom into quarters and add it along with the olive oil into a small pan. Use medium-high heat until there is a little sizzle and then add the frozen peas. Stir with a spoon adding salt and pepper. Turn down low and continue cooking for another 3 to 4 minutes. Stir one last time and then plate.

TIP: If you want to add a little more flavor to this, add a small amount of white wine and let it cook off before serving.

Sautéed Baby Spinach & Garlic

I find this side of vegetables to be one of the most fulfilling and delicious. It is full of umami. You can turn it into a full dinner by stirring in cooked penne pasta, adding more olive oil (enough so pasta is shiny), and serving it with plenty of Parmesan on top. As with all of the recipes with mushrooms, if someone prefers not to eat them just leave them out of their serving.

Ingredients

Baby Spinach

2-3 tbsp Extra Virgin Olive Oil

2-3 Cloves of Garlic

3-4 Mushrooms

Salt & Pepper

1/2 Cup of White Wine

Tools

Cast iron pan or any pan you have, paring knife, cutting board, wooden spatula

Prepare

Clean mushrooms and slice. Remove skins from garlic cloves and chop each clove into decently small pieces. Add olive oil to pan and add in the mushrooms and garlic. Cook on medium-high heat until mushrooms start to brown and garlic gets soft. Once garlic is soft, use spatula to smash down any pieces you can on the bottom of the pan to pulverize them. Add 3 to 4 big handfuls of baby spinach into the pan, then add the wine. Cook until the spinach wilts completely and is soft. When you plate it, there should be a little broth to accompany each one of the servings.

TIP: After the garlic has started to cook and soften, use the wooden spatula to smash it into the pan to more evenly spread out the flavor. If garlic starts to get too brown, add a little water or white wine to deglaze it. Be sure to add a little bit of the broth to each serving. It makes all the difference in flavor.

BEVERAGES

Longevity Sipping Chocolate

Wellness Smoothie

"Pretty in Magenta" Tea

Longevity Sipping Chocolate

This is like hot chocolate except super concentrated and a very small serving. Thanks to Chef Paul Palomino on the tip for using brown sugar.

Ingredients

1 1/2 tbsp Cocoa Powder

1 tbsp Brown Sugar

1 dash Cinnamon

1 dash Turmeric

1 tsp Vanilla

1 dash Salt and Pepper

1 tbsp Filtered Water

3-4 tbsp Milk

Tools

Small stainless steel pan or any pan you have, small whisk, small silicone spatula

Prepare

Put all of the dry ingredients into a cold pan and whisk together. Turn the heat to low, add in the water, and then mix together to create a thick chocolate paste. Then add milk into the mixture until it is just thinner than syrup. Serve a small portion (about shot size) in a cup.

TIP: Use a silicon spatula so you don't lose out on any of the cocoa stuck to the pan.

Wellness Smoothie

This is a delicious way to get more fruit into the diet. It is a good addition to breakfast before school in the morning and full of healthy nutrients.

Ingredients

3 to 4 Frozen Strawberries

1/4 cup Frozen Blueberries

1/2 Frozen Banana

1/4 cup Lemon Yogurt

Splash of Juice (cherry, pomegranate, or orange)

1/2 cup Lemonade

1/2 cup "Pretty in Magenta" Tea (see next recipe)

2 Vitamin D 1000 IU Tablets

1 Triple Ginseng, 1 Reishi Mushroom, and 1 Licorice Capsule (empty and discard outer capsules)

Dash of Turmeric

Tools

blender

Prepare

Put all ingredients into blender and blend until smooth. Serve right away in a small glass.

"Pretty in Magenta" Tea

This tea was inspired by a drink at Starbucks® my daughter liked. It is thirst quenching with just the right amount of sweetness from the honey.

Ingredients

2 Tazo® Passion Tea Bags

1 Peppermint Tea Bag

1 Decaffeinated Green Tea Bag

Local Honey

Filtered Water

Tools

Small stainless steel pan or any pan you have with a lid, mason jars or beverage container, large soup spoon

Prepare

Put the tea bags into about 2 cups of water on the stove and turn to medium-high heat. After a minute or so turn the heat down to low, put the lid on, and let simmer for about 10 minutes. Turn the heat off and discard the tea bags. Use the spoon to dip into the jar of honey and let the honey drip off of the spoon without putting the spoon in the tea. Repeat this 4 to 5 times, but the last time dip the spoon into the hot tea and stir until the honey is dissolved. Fill the rest of the pan with room temperature cold water. Once the tea is cool enough, transfer to a beverage container and continue to fill with water until full. If using mason jars, fill about 2/3 full of tea mixture from pan and the rest with water. Put in refrigerator and serve chilled.

Product Recommendation

Tazo® Passion Tea

Bradshaw Honey Farms Orange Blossom Honey (Visalia, CA)

TIP: Tucking the tea bag labels up by the pan handle may help to keep them from falling into the water.

www.ingramcontent.com/pod-product-compliance
Lightning Source LLC
Chambersburg PA
CBHW041522120626
46551CB00018B/2538